SUPERKIDS

SUPERKIDS

YOUNG HEROES IN ACTION

LESLIE GARRETT

HarperCollins*Publishers*Ltd

Special thanks to the YTV Achievement Awards, the Kids Sense Safety Hero Awards, and the Reebok Human Rights Youth in Action Awards for their recognition of children's accomplishments, and for their help with this book.

http://www.harpercollins.com/canada

Canadian Cataloguing in Publication Data

Garrett, Leslie, 1964–
    Superkids : young heroes in action

ISBN 0-00-638665-2

1. Children - Biography - Juvenile literature.
2. Heroes - Biography - Juvenile literature. I. Title.

CT107.G37 1997   j920'.0083   C96-931892-8

97 98 99 ❖ WEB 10 9 8 7 6 5 4 3 2 1

Printed and bound in Canada

To my mother, without whose hard work and determination this book would not have been possible, and my father, whose stalwart support gives us both the strength to climb higher.

CONTENTS

Foreword   ix

Introduction   xi

RESCUE FROM THE FLAMES   3
    ★ Earl Okemow and Stanley Houle

RUNAWAY BUS   11
    ★ John Waldron and Jena Nokes

ON THIN ICE   19
    ★ Dustin Paterson

THE POWER OF A PLAYGROUND   25
    ★ Vanessa Ann Nelson

IN THE DRIVER'S SEAT   31
    ★ Brad McPherson

SWIMMING FOR THEIR LIVES 37
  ★ Paul Cadman and Charlie Sturgeon

A SCHOOL FOR IQBAL 45
  ★ Amanda Loos and Amy Papile

HOLD YOUR HORSES! 55
  ★ Jeremy Rosenberg

AN EAGLE FEATHER FOR AMELIA 61
  ★ Amelia Peter-Paul

HE SHOOTS, HE SCORES! 71
  ★ Michael Weber

"FIRE!" 79
  ★ Tiffiney Betts

THE FIRST OF MANY STEPS 89
  ★ Jesse Davidson

FOREWORD

BY ERIC WILSON

Dear Kids:

I'm glad you've decided to read these stories about some SuperKids who have dared to make our world a better place.

Life is great, but it's not perfect. We look around and see injustice. How do we deal with this? Some people throw up their hands and walk away, but others don't. They're the true heroes — the ones who take a stand.

In this book, Leslie Garrett tells us about ordinary kids who had the courage to help others in many different ways. Some performed heroic rescues, while others fought against injustice. As a result, kids in one city have safe playgrounds now; elsewhere, there are children who no longer live in slavery because of the actions of those who were determined to help.

Because I write books for children, sometimes people ask me, "Why don't you write for adults?" I reply, "I already do — they're just not adults yet." You are the future leaders and the future parents, so it's a great honour for me as an author to have some input into your thoughts and attitudes. Each of us is born with goodness in our heart, so writing for kids enables me to encourage you always to believe in the power of good.

The proof of what kids can accomplish is found in the following stories. As I read them, I felt such pride in your generation. Each of you is a SuperKid, and I look forward with excitement and optimism to the world you will build.

Eric Wilson

INTRODUCTION

I've thought a lot since beginning this book about what exactly a hero is. A hero is someone brave, I've decided, someone strong, someone who works hard for what he or she believes in. The kids in this book are certainly all those things. What's remarkable is that these heroes are ordinary kids — just like you. Some are shy, some are outgoing; some are brimming with self-confidence, others struggle with self-doubt. But all of them have it within them to do something incredible.

As I've listened to their stories, I've been awed and amazed. I've also been humbled. Without exception, these kids have performed their heroic deeds — whether rescuing a brother or sister from a burning house, raising money to fight a frightening disease, or offering child slaves an education — with single-minded dedication.

When faced with scary and sometimes overwhelming decisions, they never took the easy way out.

I've learned a lot from these young heroes. I've learned that hard work is worth it. I've learned that small people can bring about huge change. Talking with these young people has convinced me that our world will be in good hands.

These young people have also changed me. And that is what I think a hero really is — someone who makes us better people just because we know them, someone who helps us find the best in ourselves. Some heroes have books written about them. Others make their marks on the world quietly and without recognition. I thank the young heroes in this book for letting me into their lives and for letting me tell their stories. I feel proud and privileged to have played a part.

Leslie Garrett
February 1997
London, Ontario

SUPERKIDS

RESCUE FROM THE FLAMES

In the small native community of Peerless Lake, Alberta, the winter is cold and long. Snow covers the ground and roofs of the small houses from October through April — and sometimes even May. But that's just fine for Earl Okemow and his good friend Stanley Houle. The two Grade 4 classmates at Peerless Lake School love to play street hockey.

"Hey, Stanley," said Earl one Thursday in February 1995. "Want to come over after school and play hockey?" Later that day, just as they had on countless other days, the boys bundled up and headed outdoors for a game in front of Earl's small bungalow.

Just a short distance from the Okemows' home is the community's central pumphouse. With no

STANLEY HOULE   EARL OKEMOW

TOM SANDLER PHOTOGRAPHY

running water in their houses, families must go to the pumphouse to get water. "Earl," Josephine Okemow called to her son as she walked from the house to her truck, "I'm going to get water. I'll just be a couple of minutes, but keep an eye on your little brother and sister for me."

"Okay," said Earl, waving good-bye. As Earl's mother drove off down the street, the two eight-year-olds picked up their game where they'd left off.

A few minutes later, they were startled by a sudden loud sound. *Thump. Thump. Thump.* The noise was coming from Earl's house. Earl and Stanley turned to see what was happening. There in the window was Earl's five-year-old brother Bradley, his eyes wide with terror. "Help me!" he was yelling through the glass. And, as the two boys watched in horror, flames began to climb the curtains.

They ran to the front door and pushed it open. Huddled together on top of the coffee table in the living room were Bradley and his baby sister, 11-month-old Serena, surrounded by flames and smoke. The roar of the fire was deafening. Although Earl and Stanley could see the terrified children, they couldn't get to them. Heat and smoke overwhelmed the two boys and forced them back outside.

On the front step, they gulped in the cold fresh air. "Take your jacket off and fill it with snow," ordered Stanley. He figured that wet jackets held over their heads wouldn't burn as easily and might help protect them from the smoke.

Earl quickly obeyed, tearing off his coat and frantically filling it with snow. "Help me, Earl!" Bradley cried desperately from inside. "Help me!" Earl grabbed his snow-filled jacket, held it above his head and over his mouth, and ran back into the burning house.

In the smoke-filled living room, fire raced up and down the curtains. Earl pulled wildly at them, hoping that he could stomp out the flames and get the fire under control. But, to his horror, the flames leapt to the sleeves of his jacket. He slapped at the sleeves with his hands and managed to put out the flames, but the rest of the fire was spreading too quickly for him to stop it.

Both Bradley and Serena still huddled on top of the coffee table. Flames licked at them and the smoke surrounded them like a thick fog. Earl picked up his baby sister first and struggled back to the front door where Stanley was waiting, just outside. Earl handed Serena to his friend and turned back into the house. With the crying infant held tightly to his chest, Stanley raced next door to Dwayne Muskwa's house. "Fire!" he hollered, pounding on Dwayne's door. "There's a fire at Earl's house!"

Fighting his way through the heat and smoke, Earl found Bradley was still standing on the coffee table, crying and coughing. *Crash!* Down went the television set as the stand supporting it burned away. Grabbing Bradley's hand, Earl led his terrified brother from the house.

Once outside, the two brothers tried to catch their breath, then they, too, headed over to Dwayne Muskwa's house. Dwayne, hearing Stanley's cry for help, had come outside to see what was going on. Still holding Serena, Stanley pointed towards the Okemow house. "Fire," he told Dwayne. "At Earl's." By the time Dwayne had hurried next door, flames had completely engulfed the Okemow house. Seeing Earl and Bradley safely making their way towards him, Dwayne said a silent thanks that the Okemow children were all right.

Word of the fire spread quickly in the small community and soon a crowd gathered. Men dipped buckets into neighbours' water barrels and ran with them to douse the fire. But the blaze roared on.

From Dwayne's house, Stanley spotted Josephine Okemow returning home in her truck. He ran into the street and flagged her down. Sobbing, he told her that her house was on fire. Josephine burst into tears and, her voice shaking, said, "Where are my children?"

"They're okay," Stanley told her. Then he returned to the neighbour's, exhausted and sad.

Josephine ran to her house, but it was too late. The buckets of water couldn't keep the blaze in check and the fire was burning out of control. In moments, the Okemows' home was reduced to smouldering ashes.

Although the Okemows were left homeless, it was thanks to the bravery of Earl and Stanley that Bradley and Serena didn't die in the fire. To recognize their bravery, the principal at Peerless Lake School nominated the two boys for a YTV Achievement Award. Each year, YTV, a children's television station, sponsors achievement awards recognizing remarkable youth in a number of different categories, including sports, writing, public service, and bravery. After considering many compelling stories, the judges chose Earl and Stanley as winners in the bravery category. The two boys and their parents were flown to Toronto, where they spent a wonderful week that they wished could last forever. They accepted their award in front of a huge audience at the televised awards ceremony. The two boys, who had chosen to dress in the same outfit — a gift from Roots Canada — spoke humbly of their accomplishment. "I'm just glad we could save Bradley and Serena," said Stanley.

Back in Peerless Lake, Earl and Stanley are still good friends. They still love to play hockey on winter afternoons. And they still think of that wonderful week in Toronto — not only because they won the YTV Achievement Award, but because they got to watch a hockey practice of the Toronto Maple Leafs. For two young hockey fans from Peerless Lake, it was a dream come true.

RUNAWAY BUS

April 29, 1996, was a grey, drizzly day in Knox, Indiana.

John Waldron, a quiet, fair-haired 17-year-old, sat talking with his young friend Matt at the back of the school bus, which was idling just outside the town's only high school.

Jena Nokes, a dark-haired 15-year-old, stepped up onto the bus. She nodded to the bus driver, a substitute who had been driving the route for only about three weeks, and then walked halfway down the aisle. She swung her tall, lean frame into an empty seat, ignoring her three younger brothers and younger sister, who were sitting with their friends. *They can be such pains,* thought Jena to herself. She usually didn't take

JOHN WALDRON   **JENA NOKES**

the bus, but today she'd decided to skip swim practice and head home. She just wasn't in the mood for practising her scissors kick. She barely noticed John Waldron sitting a few rows behind her at the back, even though he was her neighbour and the only other high school student on the bus.

At 3:05 p.m., the school bus pulled away, loaded with about two dozen elementary school students, and John and Jena. John continued chatting with his friend while Jena settled in for the 45-minute ride to her family's home.

The bus bumped along its usual route through the small town towards the outskirts, where most of the children lived. When the driver rolled past the first drop-off point, the younger kids immediately chorused, "You missed a stop!" John called to them, "He knows where he's going." But Jena, watching the driver in the rearview mirror, wasn't so sure. *There's something odd about his eyes,* she thought. And there had been rumours around school that he had epilepsy, which Jena knew sometimes causes seizures.

She tried to relax, staring out the rain-spattered window at the endless fields and rows of trees. But when the bus sped through an intersection, narrowly missing a car and passing another school bus so quickly that it looked like a yellow blur, she turned quickly to John at the back of the bus.

"Go to the bus driver and see what's wrong," she hollered over the noise of the kids, who were loudly wondering why the driver wasn't making his usual stops. *This bus is travelling far too fast,* thought John, and he began to make his way up the aisle. He held on tight to the backs of the seats to keep his balance as the bus veered crazily from one side of the street to the other.

"What's wrong?" he asked when he reached the driver, kneeling down to keep his balance and shouting over the noise of the racing engine. No response. The bus sped on, missed a curve in the road, and swerved onto a muddy dirt track through a farmer's field. Alarmed, John tried again. "Are you okay?" he asked the driver urgently. Still no response. The driver's face was completely blank, his eyes staring straight ahead — a look that frightened John even more.

Just then, the bus smacked into a large branch, ripping it from the tree. Startled, John raised his head and looked out the front window. "Oh no," he whispered, and felt a scream rise in his throat. Ahead was a creek — and they were charging straight for it!

John could hear the kids screaming and crying behind him, but the noise sounded strangely far away. Suddenly, the left tires of the bus hit a narrow bridge. Screeching horribly, with right wheels dangling over the edge, the bus tore across, ripping off bridge planks as it went. All the kids could do was hang on. John shut his eyes and said a silent prayer.

Seconds later, the bus lurched onto the other side of the creek and rammed into one of the large cement blocks used along the shore to prevent flooding and erosion. The front of the bus leapt into the air, tossing some of the children right out of their seats. Jena's nine-year-old brother Tim bounced so high he hit his leg on the ceiling and flipped over. Then the wheels hit the ground again with a thud, and the bus rushed on.

Straight ahead, John saw forest and another river. *I'd better do something,* he thought, *and fast!* He yanked the driver's foot off the gas pedal, pressed the brake down with his right hand, and threw the gear shift into "neutral" with his left.

Finally, the bus came to a stop. The kids scrambled into the aisle, anxious to get off. The front door was jammed shut, so Jena crawled over the seats to the back, threw open the emergency door, and began helping two dozen crying and scared children off the bus. Her heart pounded with fear, but she knew the kids were counting on her to stay calm. Two little girls panicked and tried to run away, but Jena did her best to keep everyone quiet and still while she figured out how to help those who were hurt. Her brother Tim, fortunately, was fine. However, another child had bitten through his tongue and was bleeding massively out of his nose and mouth.

In the meantime, John had grabbed the bus driver's CB radio and was calling for help. Finally, the school principal answered his call. "Where are you?" the principal asked. John looked around helplessly. "I'm not sure," he responded. But, luckily, the other school bus they had passed had also radioed for help and had given proper directions. Across the barren fields, the kids could see the flashing lights of the approaching emergency vehicles. Less than three minutes later, an ambulance, fire truck, and police car all arrived. Seven children were loaded into the ambulance for the trip to the hospital, while another bus was called to transport those who weren't as badly hurt. John rode in the ambulance with a terrified little girl who wanted him to stay with her.

When they arrived at the hospital, the bus driver and all his passengers were carefully checked out. Surprisingly, there were few injuries, and both John and Jena were fine. The small hospital soon became chaotic — overrun with concerned parents, scared kids, and busy doctors and nurses. Jena waited with her sister and brothers for their dad, who had heard about the accident and was coming to pick them up. Meanwhile, John went from child to child, doing what he could to comfort each of them. When his parents arrived, they were relieved to find that he was okay — in fact, he was watching cartoons with the frightened little girl on his lap.

When the local sheriff approached John and asked to speak with him about the accident, John told him the terrifying tale. He repeated his story to a reporter with the local paper. Then, finally, he left for home for the second time that day — this time, with his parents.

The next morning, many of the children waited nervously for the school bus. John refused a ride from his mom and climbed onto the bus with the rest of the kids. And, two stops later, there was one little girl who would only get on if she could sit beside John Waldron — her hero.

ON THIN ICE

Eleven-year-old Dustin Paterson likes to watch television. He says he knows that too much TV will rot his brain. But no one can argue that Dustin's television-watching just may have saved his friend Adam's life.

Dustin and Adam James — better known as A.J. — were visiting the small town of Fernie, British Columbia, in March 1996 for a hockey tournament as members of the Calgary Seven Clubs Atom 1 Thunder. Dustin plays right wing on the team, while A.J. plays left wing.

The two boys were in a hotel room with their mothers when they decided to go for a walk. They had a few hours until their evening game and were getting restless, so they bundled up into their winter

DUSTIN PATERSON

jackets, scarves, hats, and gloves. When they got outside, they were glad they'd dressed warmly. Although the temperature wasn't below freezing, there was a cold wind blowing from the north.

Dustin and A.J. decided to wander down towards Elk River. They both had hockey on their minds, and they talked about their team's chances in the hockey tournament. Even though the Seven Clubs Thunder was competing against 11 of the best teams from British Columbia and Alberta, Dustin, A.J., and their teammates had won the two previous games. Both boys were sure they would win again when they played that night.

When they reached a small, narrow branch of the river, A.J. started to walk out on the ice. "Don't do that, A.J.," Dustin said anxiously. "The ice doesn't look very thick." But A.J. confidently kept walking, sure that the ice could support his light weight. "Stop!" Dustin cried again. But it was too late. With a sharp crack, the thin ice split and A.J. crashed through, right in the middle of the river.

"Help!" he called out to Dustin on the shore.

"Can you stand up, A.J.?" shouted Dustin, hoping the water wasn't over his friend's head.

"No," A.J. cried. "Help!" Desperately, he tried to

pull himself out of the water, but the ice kept breaking all around him.

Dustin knew he had to think quickly. He looked around but saw no one. He knew that he should run for help. But the water was cold and deep, and he wasn't sure his friend would survive if he didn't get him out of the river fast.

He suddenly thought back to an episode of the television show *Rescue 911*. A group of snowmobilers was racing along the frozen surface of a big river when one of the snowmobiles went through the ice, taking the driver with it. Dustin remembered that the rescuer got down on his stomach and slid across the ice to his friend. Dustin knew that lying down let the rescuer distribute his weight over a wider area, so that the ice could support him.

Scared but determined, Dustin decided to rescue A.J. himself.

He hooked one foot around a rock near the shore. That way, Dustin figured, when he was pulling A.J., he wouldn't get dragged in, too. Then he got down on his stomach and stretched out to where A.J. was still clinging to the ice to keep his head above water. Dustin was lucky that his friend was smaller and much lighter. When A.J. grabbed his arm, Dustin gripped his friend's soaking sleeve and pulled as hard as he could. The ice cracked under the weight of the two boys, but they quickly dropped onto their bellies and slithered carefully to the safety of the shore. In a matter of seconds, A.J. was out of danger.

But he wasn't out of the cold. Soaked to the skin, A.J. was shivering violently, and his fingers were getting stiff. Dustin did his best to wring out A.J.'s soaking wet pants and jacket. Then the two boys, cold and shaken, ran as fast as they could back to the hotel.

"Were you guys playing in puddles again?" asked Dustin's mom when the boys stumbled into the hotel room. But in a split second, she and A.J.'s mother realized that A.J. didn't just have wet feet — his heavy coat was sopping wet and his face was red as a beet. They hurried him out of his clothes and ordered him into a warm bath. Meanwhile, the boys filled their mothers in on what had happened. *Thank goodness both boys didn't fall through,* Dustin's mother thought to herself. *Who would have rescued them then?*

After A.J. got out of his bath, the two boys sat

quietly and watched TV in the hotel. In spite of their terrifying afternoon, both boys insisted they could play hockey that night. And play they did, each scoring a goal and helping their team win a third game in the tournament.

When Dustin and A.J. returned to their home-town of Calgary, it didn't take long for word to get out about Dustin's heroic action. His aunt phoned the *Calgary Sun* and soon the awards for his quick thinking and bravery began pouring in. Dustin won an award from his hockey arena, one from the Calgary Police Service, and one from Kids Sense, a national program sponsored by the International Council of Shopping Centres that recognizes child safety heroes.

Now, when someone tells Dustin that television is bad for him, he simply smiles. He knows that sometimes television saves lives.

THE POWER OF A PLAYGROUND

Vanessa Ann Nelson considers herself lucky. The 12-year-old from Oakland, California, loves playgrounds and has always had access to a safe one. In fact, her father, John Nelson, designs children's playgrounds and designed the one at Vanessa's school, Crocker Highlands Elementary.

Vanessa learned through Project Playground, part of Nike's PLAY (Participate in the Lives of American Youth) program, that some children weren't so lucky. In fact, playground equipment at 58 Oakland schools had been closed to kids since 1993. Following a tragic playground accident at one school, in which a young child died after falling off equipment onto unsafe matting, inspectors discovered that protection underneath

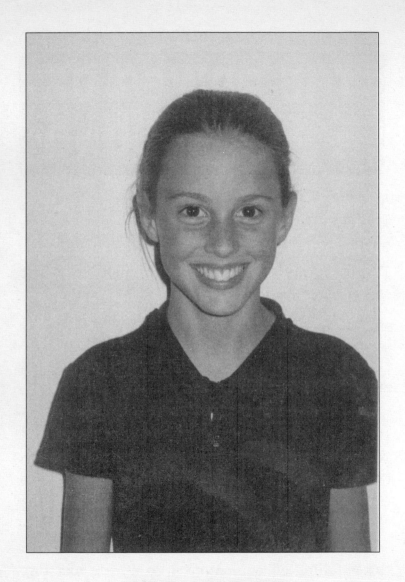

VANESSA ANN NELSON

many of the structures was unfit.

Vanessa's father was involved with Project Playground, along with a woman named NZ Carol. They began looking for an official "spokeskid" to travel to schools and events and talk about the need for safe playground structures. They first approached Vanessa's 15-year-old sister Julia. "But she didn't want to do it," explains Vanessa. "I was hoping they'd ask me. I began to realize how poor many of the structures were. And I realized how lucky my school was." Vanessa was eager to change things for the better. When they asked her to take on the job as spokeskid, she had her chance.

Nike's Project Playground works with other big companies, such as Foot Locker, to rebuild play areas for kids in Oakland. The more involved Vanessa got in the project, the more aware she became of how dangerous some of the playgrounds were. At one school she visited, she was shocked to see a playground structure with no padding underneath it, only cement. Because the play area was in such bad repair, it had been blocked off with yellow "caution" tape — a sight that made Vanessa very sad. She also noticed a trend: the poorer the neighbourhood, the lousier the playground. She became determined that every school in Oakland — in every part of the city, no matter how poor — would have the safe structure that her school was lucky enough to have.

As part of her responsibility as spokeskid, Vanessa had to give speeches at schools. At some, she spoke to children, but at most she addressed adults — principals, teachers, school board officials. She was very nervous at first, and wasn't sure people would listen to her. "Having a kid up there on stage is different from having an adult," says Vanessa. "I was afraid that people wouldn't listen because I was a kid." She needn't have worried. With the audience members listening intently and slowly nodding their heads at her words, Vanessa discovered early on that her message was being heard.

Soon Vanessa was in demand as a speaker at many Oakland-area schools and occasionally on television. She spoke compellingly of the need for safe playgrounds, and found that her words were getting results. She also told her audiences that they could help by donating old running shoes to the cause. Nike had promised to recycle any old Nike sneakers taken to Foot Locker stores into matting for underneath the structures. In the end, 200,000 shoes were transformed into protective surfaces for playgrounds.

One night a few months later, Vanessa was attending an Oakland Warriors basketball game when a voice called her name over the loudspeaker and invited her out onto the court. With shaking knees, she made her way into the bright lights and was presented with a certificate and plaque acknowledging her hard work on behalf of children in Oakland.

Today, Vanessa's work with Project Playground has pretty much wound up. She plans on taking a look at the result of all her efforts — the safe new playgrounds that children now enjoy in many of the city's schools.

Her year in the spotlight has given Vanessa some bright ideas about her future. Next on the determined 12-year-old's list? Hollywood, where she plans to become an actress.

IN THE DRIVER'S SEAT

The people of Surrey, British Columbia, see a lot of dark, rainy days and November 2, 1995, was no exception. At 2:30 p.m., 12-year-old Brad McPherson was just leaving class at Senator Reid Elementary School. He walked past the school office and down the hall, where the equipment was kept for the school crossing guards.

The Grade 7 student slipped on his reflector vest, not bothering to do up the ties, grabbed his big stop sign, and headed out into the drizzle to the intersection of 92nd and 126th streets, where he worked with another crossing guard.

It was always busy right after school, and Brad was conscientiously getting a group of kindergarten children and their moms across the street

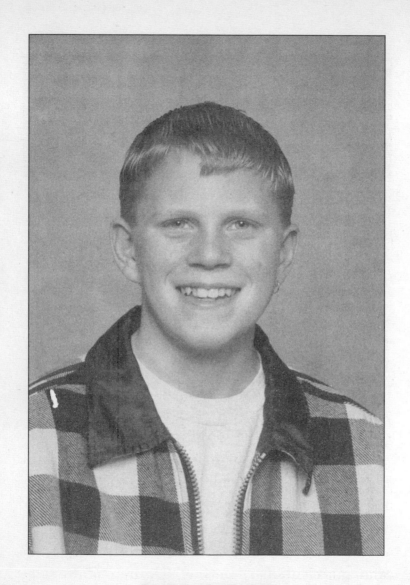

BRAD MCPHERSON

safely to their waiting cars. A lot of cars were idling on the slick road outside the school as parents waited for sons and daughters to appear. Brad noticed one small grey car in particular. Other cars were honking because the driver had simply stopped in the middle of the road, partway down a slight hill — making it difficult for other cars to pass. Brad was even more surprised when the driver simply got out of the car and headed into the school. *That's pretty strange,* Brad thought to himself. *He's left three small kids alone in the car.*

Brad carried on with his duties, but he kept an eye on that small grey car.

With their father gone, the three small children in the car began jumping around. When the little boy hopped into the driver's seat, he accidentally moved the gear shift out of "park." The grey car began slowly rolling down the hill.

A few students had gathered at Brad's corner to cross. As he always did, Brad looked up and down the street to make sure no cars were coming through the intersection. That was when he saw something very frightening: the grey car was coming straight for him and he couldn't see anyone in the driver's seat.

In a split second, Brad had ripped off his bulky vest, thrown down his stop sign, and started racing towards the driverless car. He had one thought in his head: *I've got to stop this car so no one will get hurt.*

Only when he got closer did he see that the three young children were still inside. Breathless, he reached the runaway car, which was picking up speed towards the busy intersection. People's curious gazes turned to looks of horror as they realized what was happening. Brad grabbed the handle and tried to open the driver's door. *Oh no,* he thought in a panic, *it's locked.* Fortunately, the window was down, so Brad reached in and lifted the lock. When he tried the door again, it swung open. "Move over," Brad ordered the small boy in the driver's seat. To the two children in the back seat, Brad barked, "Sit down and keep quiet." His heart pounding as the car rolled towards the intersection, Brad slammed his foot on the brakes, hit the emergency brake, and then put the car in "park." The car lurched to a stop.

A teenager who had been in a van parked behind the car reached it seconds after Brad had brought it to a halt. "Are you okay?" he asked.

"Yeah," Brad answered, although he wasn't so sure. His heart was pounding and he felt kind of panicky.

Just as Brad was getting out of the car, the driver arrived. Without a word, the man simply got into the automobile and pulled away. Speechless and still shaken, Brad watched in disbelief as the grey car disappeared.

In the meantime, some of the parents who had seen Brad's quick action rushed over to him and offered their congratulations. Some of the other crossing guards had gathered as well, and were talking excitedly about what had happened. Brad joined in eagerly, but after a few minutes he went back to his job of getting schoolchildren safely across the street — like a true professional.

When their shift was over, the crossing guards headed for the principal's office. They had been instructed to report any problems that occurred when they were on duty, so they told Brad's tale to the principal. After listening to Brad, the principal congratulated him on such an act of courage. After the children left, he called Brad's mother at home to tell her that her son's quick thinking had probably saved the lives of three small children.

Brad ran home a little faster than usual that afternoon. He couldn't wait to tell his mom about what had happened, unaware that news of his heroic act had already reached her.

Word spread quickly in the community, too. The city of Surrey was very proud of their young hero. There was an assembly at school to honour Brad's bravery. He received an award from the safety patrol for the school and a YTV Achievement Award. He was also given a Kids Sense Safety Award, which recognizes courage and common sense in children who, through their quick thinking, prevent tragedies. Brad also received many letters from people who wanted to congratulate the young hero. Some fans even offered him money and gifts.

Today, Brad is in high school and no longer a crossing guard. But he may just have a future as a superhero. "I felt proud of myself that I'd saved those kids. It felt good inside," he says. "I'd do it again, no problem. If I saw someone drowning, I'd jump in and save them, too."

SWIMMING FOR THEIR LIVES

Blue skies. Warm sunshine. June 21, 1996, was the perfect day to celebrate the end of the school year. That's exactly what three Grade 8 classes from Lorne Avenue Public School in London, Ontario, were doing along the bank of the Thames River in Springbank Park. After enjoying a picnic lunch, students were having water fights, tossing a football, and just goofing around.

Fifteen-year-old Paul Cadman, 14-year-old Charlie Sturgeon, and six of their friends decided to pool their money and rent two aluminum rowboats from a kiosk at the edge of the river. Laughing and talking, they put on their lifejackets and climbed into the boats. With two hours before the boats had to be returned, the eight

CHARLIE STURGEON   **PAUL CADMAN**

friends set off on the river for some fun.

Trying to row the boats created lots of laughter. The river was particularly high after a wet spring and there was a strong current. As a result, no one could seem to get the boats going properly.

Charlie and his girlfriend, 14-year-old Tasha Stevenson, were rowing one boat with 13-year-old Tanya Whaling and 14-year-old Crystal George on board. While Tasha and Charlie struggled to get their boat going in a straight line, Paul, with 14-year-olds Amber Sturdy, Serena Bovin, and Clint Walker in his boat, had managed to get way ahead. Unfortunately, none of the teens in Paul's boat was paying much attention to where the current was carrying them — and by the time someone noticed the roar of water rushing over the dam, the boat was dangerously close to it.

Charlie's rowboat was still a fair distance behind Paul's when he heard the two girls in Paul's boat screaming over the sound of the rushing water. "Stay back!" they yelled at Charlie and Tasha. "Stay back!" Their boat was teetering on the edge of the dam. Paul was rowing frantically, but the current was too strong.

From their boat, Charlie, Tasha, Tanya, and Crystal watched as their four friends leapt out of their rowboat just seconds before it disappeared over the dam. In horror, they saw Amber, then Clint, and then Serena get swept over behind the boat. Only Paul remained visible, swimming furiously against the current.

"Tasha, take the oars," commanded Charlie, and he jumped into the water. "C'mon, man. Swim!" he yelled to his friend. "Paul, you can do it!" He swam towards his friend, trying desperately to reach Paul, who was swimming as hard as he could. But his tired friend couldn't match the strength of the current. As Charlie watched helplessly, Paul was swept over the dam.

Out of Charlie's sight, his four friends miraculously surfaced on the other side. They were scared, but alive. Somehow, they had managed to avoid hitting any rocks as they were pulled over, and their good fortune probably saved their lives. A quick-thinking bystander immediately threw a fishing line that caught Clint's shirt, and pulled the teenager to safety on the shore.

But Paul, Amber, and Serena weren't out of danger yet. All three were in the middle of the river, quite a distance from the shore. The two girls were exhausted and couldn't find the strength to swim to safety. Amber was in the worst shape — paralysed with fear and barely able to stay afloat.

Paul swam over to the two girls. "Serena, climb on my back," he ordered. Then he put his arms under Amber to support her. With Serena on his back, Paul let the current carry all three of them to a tree on a small island in the middle of the river. Because the river was so high, the island was about half a metre under water. But the tree offered safety — at least for the moment. The girls stood in the knee-deep water and clung to the slender trunk as the current swept past their legs. The tiny tree clearly couldn't support all three of them, so Paul swam to another tree near-by. The current was even more powerful there, and he had to hold on tightly to save himself from the rushing water. Paul watched hopefully as people began to gather on the shore. Word of the accident had spread quickly.

"Is everyone okay?" called out one of the teachers.

"Yeah, everyone's okay," Paul yelled back.

Meanwhile, on the other side of the dam,

Charlie had no idea what had happened to his friends. He had grabbed onto a metal bar attached to the concrete wall and tried to catch his breath. But when he looked back to his own boat, he saw that it had edged perilously close to the dam. While Tasha tried valiantly to row against the current, the others were screaming and crying. Mustering up his strength, Charlie swam over to where the rowboat hovered, only about a metre and a half from the rushing water-falls. He choked on some water and began cough-ing, but managed to talk to the girls in his boat. "Be quiet," he pleaded over the roar of the dam. "Calm down and sit still."

"Get in, Charlie," they yelled back. "Get in the boat!" Tanya had taken over the oars because Tasha was too tired. With all his energy, Charlie managed to push the boat towards the concrete wall, away from the current. *How long will I be able to hold it here?* he asked himself anxiously, exhausted from the effort.

Suddenly, he realized that they weren't alone. All over the dam above them, people were wait-ing to help. One friend managed to grab the chain attached to the rowboat and held it tight. Then, one by one, the terrified teens climbed up the side of the dam until strong arms could reach down and pull them up onto solid ground. They hugged each other in relief. When someone told them that Paul, Amber, and Serena were still in the water, they headed to shore where they could see their three friends.

A rescue crew in a rubber boat with a small motor set off from the shore to save Paul, Amber, and Serena. As the boat neared Paul, he waved them on. "Go get the girls first," he told the crew, knowing that Amber needed medical attention fast. When the rescue boat reached the two girls, the crew helped them on and wrapped the shivering teens in blankets. The boat then picked up Paul and took them all to shore.

Ambulances were waiting to take all of the students to hospital. Ambulance attendants placed Amber on a spinal board, fearing she'd seriously injured her back. "You'll be okay," whispered Tanya, as Amber cried softly. Miraculously, all the students were released from the hospital later that day. Except for some cuts and bruises, they were okay. And thanks to Paul Cadman, Charlie Sturgeon, and some quick-thinking rescuers, the eight friends had more to celebrate a few days later than simply graduating from elementary school.

A SCHOOL FOR IQBAL

Nothing could have prepared Amanda Loos and Amy Papile for the shock they received on December 2, 1994. When Iqbal Masih, a former child slave from Pakistan, walked into Ron Adams's Grade 7 class at Broad Meadows Middle School in Quincy, Massachusetts, the two 12-year-olds, along with the rest of the class, couldn't help stare. It wasn't the nasty scar above his eyebrow. It wasn't the way he chomped his gum with so much pleasure. What was so alarming to the students was that this boy who was their age was so tiny.

"We were all talking," remembers Amanda. "Then, when Iqbal walked in with his translator, everybody's head turned to look. The room became so silent. It was a teacher's dream."

AMANDA LOOS

AMY PAPILE

Reebok
Human
Rights
Award

RICHARD SOBOL

The students had been warned that Iqbal's appearance would be surprising. The boy had been sold into slavery at the age of four to a carpet manufacturer. For the next six years, he had been chained to a loom for more than 12 hours a day, tying tiny knots in carpets. He escaped at the age of 10, but the years of malnutrition and abuse had stunted his growth. Now 12 years old, he looked to the class like a child of 6 or 7. "When he sat down on a chair in the cafeteria later that day," says Amanda, "his little feet swung way above the ground."

In spite of his small size, Iqbal's voice was strong. And the message he brought the students was stronger still. He told them that child slavery continues to exist in many countries and that it must be stopped.

Like many people, the students at Broad Meadows Middle School believed that slavery had disappeared long ago. Now a child their own age was proof that it still existed and that something had to be done.

They took him to the cafeteria for lunch, but he didn't like the food and chose to eat plain rice. "When he finished eating," says Amanda, "we showered him with gifts," including the chewing gum he so clearly loved. "At that moment," she recalls, "watching his tiny hands open all the presents, I realized that this is how children should be treated." Together, Amy, Amanda, and the rest of the students decided to take action.

A few of them gathered to discuss what they could do. Some began calling carpet stores in their hometown to ask storeowners where they got their rugs and what their policy was on carpets made using child labour. The kids were often told — not too politely — to mind their own business. But that didn't stop them. Next, they began a letter-writing campaign. Within three days, the students had produced 670 letters to storeowners and politicians, including 400 for Iqbal to take back to Pakistan, asking Prime Minister Benazir Bhutto to do something about child labour in her country.

On December 5, 1994, Iqbal received the Reebok Human Rights Youth in Action Award at the Apollo Theater in Harlem, New York. The award recognizes young people who have worked hard on behalf of human rights around the world. Some students from Broad Meadows, including Amy and Amanda, were in the audience, waiting to deliver their bag of letters personally to Iqbal.

As they watched the young boy accept the prestigious medal, the students vowed to continue to help him fight his battle.

Working together before and after school, during lunch and on holidays, the students produced flyers to educate people about the issue of child labour. They circulated petitions to abolish the practice. They advised people to ask storeowners about the products they bought to make sure the products weren't made by child slaves. They got the mayor of Quincy involved, contacted United States senators, and wrote to world leaders.

But on April 16, 1995, while the students were enjoying their week-long spring vacation, they learned some horrifying news. Twelve-year-old Iqbal had been murdered while riding his bike in Pakistan. When Amanda heard, she thought the story was a cruel joke. Amy's mother broke the news to her daughter. All the students were shocked and very sad.

When Ron Adams saw how devastated the children were, he opened the school and organized a small memorial service for their young hero. He thought the gathering would be an appropriate end to the students' campaign against child slavery.

He couldn't have been more wrong.

"That wasn't enough," Amy told him afterwards. The other students agreed. They decided to draw up a plan to carry on Iqbal's crusade. Ron Adams, constantly amazed at his students' dedication, promised to help them in any way he could.

Then Amy came up with a daring idea. "The thought that kept Iqbal going when he was a slave," she said to her friends, classmates, and teacher, "was that someday he'd be free and in school." Then she told them all of her idea to raise money to build a school near Iqbal's hometown in Pakistan. The students thought it was a wonderful idea. Ron Adams wasn't sure they could do it, but he knew better than to underestimate his students. "Take this idea home," he told them, "and write out the steps that we will need to take — starting tomorrow."

That's exactly what they did. By the next morning, Amy had her plan. The students would contact as many other schools as they could using the class's one computer. They would send out Iqbal's story and ask others to help their cause by donating $12 — an amount chosen because it was Iqbal's age when he visited the school, his age when he received his award from Reebok, and his age when he died.

Amanda and another classmate stayed after school and wrote a wonderful letter outlining the plan. Off it went to 36 other middle schools in 30 different states. A few days later, a dozen schools in 10 states had responded, offering support and donations. A network grew — student to student, school to school, state to state, country to country.

By contacting non-governmental agencies that build schools in developing countries, the students got some estimates of how much money they needed for their plan. They set a goal of $5,000 — an amount that would cover the cost of building a one-room schoolhouse out of mud and brick, large enough to educate 20 children. Before they knew it, they'd already met and surpassed their goal. They raised it to $12,500 — an amount that would cover the cost of a two-room schoolhouse built out of mud and brick, large enough to educate 40 kids.

Twice more they reached and raised their goal. Finally, they set a target of $50,000 — an amount that would cover the cost of a four-room community education centre to educate adults as well as children.

What happened next was a wonderful surprise. Almost one year after Iqbal's visit, Ron Adams got a call from the people at Reebok. They'd been following the students' campaign quite closely and were very impressed with what they'd seen. They wanted Ron Adams's students at Broad Meadows Middle School to accept the Reebok Human Rights Youth in Action Award, one year after Iqbal had received it.

On December 5, 1995, at the Apollo Theater in Harlem, New York, Amy and Amanda were called on stage by actor Susan Sarandon to accept the award on behalf of all those involved in the campaign. Their speeches were simple and moving, and they spoke sadly of their lost friend who had taught them so much. "His feet may not have touched the floor," said Amanda, "but his words touched our hearts." Amy asked people in the audience to spread the word about the students' campaign to build a school for Iqbal. "Iqbal, dear friend, rest in peace," she said. "We haven't forgotten you."

After the ceremony, the students enjoyed meeting many celebrities. Amanda and Amy woke up the next day to discover a photograph of them being hugged by actor Richard Gere splashed on the front page of their local newspaper and carried in other papers from coast to coast.

Because of the award, the whole country learned of the students' incredible campaign. Donations and letters of support flooded in. Many people sent $12 donations, and one person even sent a cheque for $10,000. Every penny helped, and once again the students surpassed their goal.

There was only one thing to do — double their target to $100,000. The students also gave their campaign a deadline: the first anniversary of Iqbal's death on April 16, 1996.

To chart their progress, the school custodian made a giant cardboard thermometer with a goal of $100,000 at the top. Each day the thermometer showed that the students were closer to their goal. By mid-April — the deadline — they'd succeeded. A small but determined group of students from a middle school in Quincy, Massachusetts, had raised $100,100.

The students were thrilled and proud, but there was no time to celebrate. Now that they had the money, they had to find someone to build Iqbal's school.

After talking to many businesspeople, lawyers, and politicians, the students learned what their next step was. They invited groups that wanted to build Iqbal's school to submit proposals outlining how they would carry out the plan.

They received 12 proposals from all over the world — every one of them worthy of consideration. It was very difficult to choose who should get the chance to build the school, but after lots of discussion the students voted unanimously to give the project to a group from Pakistan.

Today, there's a beautiful building just outside of Iqbal's village in Pakistan that provides a place for 260 freed child slaves to learn.

Amy and Amanda, the campaign's two leaders, have moved on to high school, and a new team of students is carrying on with the project. But the two girls, now 14, continue to give speeches telling people about young Iqbal and his dream — and how a group of children from Massachusetts made it come true.

HOLD YOUR HORSES!

On November 2, 1990, 12-year-old Jeremy Rosenberg from Roberts, Wisconsin, missed his Boy Scouts meeting. "But," his mother told the Scout leader, "Jeremy has a very good reason for not attending." And she began to explain...

Jeremy loved to ride his horse over the rolling hills of the large farm that the Rosenbergs run. His grandma bought him his first horse when he was only three years old — a sturdy Shetland pony named Thunder, with a long mane and shaggy tail. He started roping (or lassoing) when he was six, and had dreams of being a cowboy.

Although Jeremy was small for his age, he was

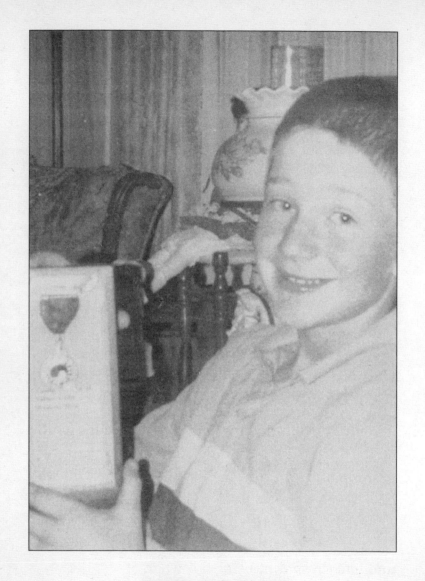

JEREMY ROSENBERG

a big help to his dad with the farm. With over one thousand cattle and some bulls on more than a thousand hectares, there was always lots to be done. He fed the cattle in the pasture, checked for sick cattle, sometimes treated sick cattle, and helped plant crops.

One early November day, Jeremy and his father were on horseback trying to separate the bulls from the cows because breeding season was over. The two Rosenbergs were roping the bulls and taking them off to a separate pasture.

Jeremy was about half a kilometre across the field from his father when he saw a strange sight. His father's horse seemed to turn a somersault and then gallop off. While Jeremy sat watching on his big quarter horse, trying to figure out what had just happened, he suddenly noticed that his father was gone. Barely stopping to think, he gave his horse a sharp kick and raced across the field. His father was nowhere to be seen. Looking around frantically, Jeremy saw a cloud of dust behind the runaway horse. At first, he thought the horse was dragging a calf that must have been caught in a rope attached to the saddle. Then the horrifying reality hit him — it was his father being dragged!

He charged after the horse, his own animal kicking up dust and stones as Jeremy urged him faster and faster. But the closer Jeremy got, the faster the other horse ran. Finally, he managed to catch up so that they were running side-by-side. He was almost too terrified to glance down, but to his great relief he saw that his father looked frightened but okay. The three layers of clothing that his father had on — long underwear, pants, and then a pair of insulated coveralls — were burned through and his skin looked scraped and sore. He had already been dragged over half a kilometre of limestone and 15-centimetre-high corn stubble.

With great skill and speed, Jeremy put his left foot into the right stirrup of his dad's horse. With his small frame stretched to the limit, he straddled the gap between the two large horses. Then he sat on the runaway horse, swung his leg over, and grabbed the reins. He pulled as hard as he could, but it was another 180 metres before the terrified horse finally came to a stop.

Jeremy's father had kept silent throughout the ordeal, knowing that if he shouted, he'd scare the horse even more. But Brad Rosenberg also knew that if Jeremy didn't keep the spooked horse still, it would break away again and run until it died from exhaustion. Finally, he spoke. "Hang onto that horse," he commanded quietly. "Don't let it bolt." Then he untangled the rope from around his legs and stood beside Jeremy, who sat gripping the reins of the trembling horse.

For a minute, the two didn't speak. Then Jeremy's dad very calmly told Jeremy to help him get the rest of the bulls out of the field. "But first," he asked, "would you go to the house and get me another pair of glasses? I've lost mine."

While his father calmed and tethered his frightened horse, Jeremy ran to the house. When he got there he called his mother, who was visiting a neighbour. He quickly told her what had happened. "I'll be right over," she told him.

Jeremy grabbed his father's second pair of glasses from on top of the refrigerator and ran back out to the field. He and his father put the last bull away in a pen apart from the cows, shut the gate, and went home, both exhausted from their ordeal.

When Debbie Rosenberg got home, she found her son and her husband sitting at the kitchen table. Although both Jeremy and his father protested that they were both fine and it wasn't such a big deal, the evidence told a different tale. Brad Rosenberg's clothes were practically in tatters and Jeremy's mom could see that they were both very shaken up.

After hearing Debbie Rosenberg's story, the Boy Scout leader was convinced that Jeremy certainly had a good reason for missing the meeting. In fact, the Boy Scouts were more than understanding. On May 14, 1991, they gave Jeremy the highest award in the organization — the Lifesaving Medal of Honor. No one was more proud than Jeremy's mom, who cried when he received the medal. Jeremy, however, thinks that rescuing people is in his blood. His great-grandfather once saved a little girl from being run over by a train. "I'm just like my great-grandpa," Jeremy said when he received his award.

After such a close call, Jeremy's mom begged him to stay away from the horses. But perhaps Jeremy was born to be a cowboy. He still rides and has even gone to a few rodeos. These days, he's content to sit on the sidelines and watch the antics. For now, anyway.

AN EAGLE FEATHER FOR AMELIA

In the spring of 1993, 11-year-old Amelia Peter-Paul received a very special gift from her mother, Barbara. It was an eagle feather — a powerful symbol of honour and courage in Amelia's native culture. She treasured the feather, unaware that in a few short months, she'd prove herself worthy of such a gift . . .

On the night of August 4, 1993, Amelia Peter-Paul was fast asleep in the guest room at her grandmother's house. Her 67-year-old grandmother, Mary Jane Jadis, lived alone just two doors down from the house where Amelia lived with her mother, father, and younger brother and

AMELIA PETER-PAUL

sister. Amelia's aunt and uncle also lived nearby.

They all lived in Scotchfort, Prince Edward Island, a quiet First Nations community of about 50 homes. In Scotchfort, everyone pretty much knew everyone else.

Amelia's culture had taught her that a deep bond exists between the generations. Elders are valued as very wise. Amelia was particularly close to her grandmother and often slept over to keep her company.

Early that morning, at around 3:30 a.m., a sudden knock at the door woke Amelia and her grandmother. "Amelia, can you answer that?" Granny called from her room. With her severe arthritis, Amelia's grandmother has trouble moving around quickly.

Amelia climbed out of bed and padded down the stairs to the back door, while her grandmother waited at the top. Outside stood a young woman Amelia recognized as a former neighbour. "I need to use your phone," she said to Amelia. Amelia stepped aside and let her in.

"You can use the one in the kitchen," Granny told her, making her way down the stairs. The young woman walked to the kitchen and made her call.

Amelia and her grandmother sat together in the living room, right next to the kitchen. They could hear the woman on the phone, and it was clear she was getting very upset. The two waited nervously as the call went on and on and the woman sounded more and more angry.

"I want to hurt somebody," she was hissing into the phone. "I want to hurt somebody." Finally, she hung up and walked into the living room.

"Who else is in the house?" the woman demanded. By this time, both Amelia and her grandmother were afraid of what this woman wanted. When they didn't answer immediately, the woman got louder. "Who else is in this house? Who else is in this house?" she repeated, her eyes blazing. They remained silent, hoping the wom-man would think they weren't alone. But the ploy didn't work. "Lock the doors and don't use the phone," the woman ordered.

Now very frightened, Amelia walked to the front door and turned the lock. Meanwhile, her grandmother's only thought was to get help. She tried to pick up the phone, hoping she could reach someone quickly.

But just as Amelia's grandmother lifted the

receiver, the woman lunged at her. She'd pulled a pair of scissors from her jeans and raised them high above Granny's head. In the blink of an eye, Amelia jumped in front of her grandmother to protect her. When the woman's arm came down, the scissors missed the older woman and tore into the back of Amelia's head. Strangely, Amelia felt nothing. Then she suddenly collapsed and fell to the ground.

Still holding the scissors, the woman lunged at Amelia's grandmother again. *I can't let anyone hurt my Granny,* thought Amelia fiercely. She struggled to get up from the floor, and managed to push her grandmother out of the way. Once again, the scissors missed their target and stabbed Amelia. Although she still didn't feel any pain, she knew she was hurt by the blood that had splattered on the walls and floor.

When the woman tried to attack Amelia's grandmother for the third time, Amelia again managed to jump up and shield her Granny from the scissors, taking the blows herself.

Then everything went black.

In a panic, the young woman ran out the door she'd come in. Amelia, conscious but dizzy, stumbled over to the stairs that led to the front door. She tried to make her way down the dozen steps, but her legs couldn't support her. She fell and lay at the bottom — dazed, confused, and bleeding. Amelia could hear the woman screaming behind the house, but couldn't understand any of her words. She felt her dog at her side, licking her wounds.

Labouring down the stairs, Granny made it to Amelia's side. The tiny woman mustered up the strength to lift her granddaughter and carry her out the door. Up a hill they struggled, past two houses on their way to Amelia's home. "Granny, I can't see," Amelia said. Since Amelia's grandmother wasn't sure where the woman had gone, she simply kept walking towards the safety of Amelia's parents. She fell once but managed to get back on her feet and support the young girl beside her.

When at last they arrived, Granny banged on the window. Her daughter — Amelia's mom — let them in.

Amelia was gasping for air, and her parents were horrified at what they saw. But there was no time for explanations. Amelia's mother was shocked at the blood and feared that Amelia was going to bleed to death. They quickly called an ambulance, the auxiliary police on the reserve, and Amelia's uncle. Amelia's father ran to the end of the street to watch for the ambulance and direct it to the house.

While she waited for help to arrive, Amelia's mom wrapped her daughter in towels and held on tightly, hoping to slow down or stop the bleeding. Granny was shaking violently and Amelia's mom talked quietly to her to calm her down.

Amelia faded in and out of consciousness.

When the ambulance pulled up, Amelia's mother got in the back with her daughter. Although Amelia's injuries were extensive, the young girl could only see a cut on her finger. All the other wounds were on her head and back.

"Fix my finger," she asked the ambulance attendants. "It hurts the most."

The trip was terrifying for Amelia's mom, who worried that they wouldn't get to the hospital quickly enough. She kept talking to Amelia, trying to keep her alert. Sometimes, Amelia's eyes would roll back in her head, and her mother would shake her back awake.

At the Queen Elizabeth Hospital in nearby Charlottetown, Amelia was rushed in. Doctors discovered that she'd been stabbed 26 times and needed many, many stitches to close her wounds. Her lungs were collapsing, so they inserted two tubes to help her get enough oxygen in her system. After a day, doctors noticed that Amelia's heart was enlarging — not a good sign. She was flown to the children's hospital in Halifax, Nova Scotia, where her parents stayed with her for three days while she recovered. Her body was still in shock from the horrifying ordeal, and she would sometimes wake up and cry. But her mother or father was always there to hold her and tell her everything was all right.

Her whole family was relieved when, after a few days, Amelia's condition improved and she was allowed to return home.

Everyone in the community had heard of Amelia's incredible act of bravery and knew that she had saved her grandmother's life. To honour her remarkable courage and strength, the people of Scotchfort celebrated Amelia at a powwow.

Since then, Amelia has received a great number of awards, both from within her community and without. As well as receiving a Governor General's Award, Amelia was thrilled to be flown to Ottawa where she accepted a YTV Achievement

Award for Bravery. While in Ottawa, Amelia, her mother, and her grandmother visited the Parliament Buildings and had dinner with some of the premiers.

Today, Amelia is a busy, determined teenager. She's a talented dancer who attends powwows all over the Maritimes, Québec, and the United States. Many people in her community see her as a role model for other young people. But Amelia has learned that being a role model brings with it a lot of responsibility — and sometimes now, three years after her ordeal, she'd prefer to be just an average 14-year-old.

It's hard for Amelia to talk about what happened that summer night in 1993. She still has some scars. But, like her memories of the terrifying attack, they are fading with time.

HE SHOOTS, HE SCORES!

It was late in the summer of 1995, but some people in the small town of Hanover, Ontario, were already thinking of the hockey season ahead. Mike Anderson, the editor of the *Hanover Post* newspaper, got together with the local cable company and the Hanover Barons hockey team to discuss televising the Junior C team's games. There was only one problem. They needed a play-by-play announcer.

About half a kilometre outside of Hanover, Michael Weber was also thinking about hockey. But, then again, he always did. During hockey season, if Michael wasn't playing hockey, he was watching it. And if he wasn't watching it, he was thinking about watching it. Whenever a friend

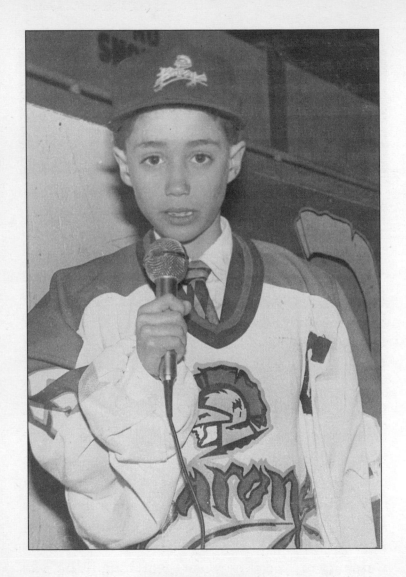

MICHAEL WEBER

invited him over, Michael always made sure he could watch the game before he accepted.

On Saturday nights, Michael and his older brother Jeff went to church, where his mother played the organ. Right after the service, Michael always tried to hurry his family out so he could get home and turn on *Hockey Night in Canada.* "No chatting, no stopping! Let's get home right away," he would urge them, dragging them to the car. When he arrived home, he'd race over to the family's television set, switch on the game, turn down the volume, and do the play-by-play himself. Every once in a while, he'd listen to the famous duo Don Cherry and Ron MacLean, learn a few of their tricks, and then try them out himself.

One day that summer, Michael's mother read a little story in the *Hanover Post* about the plans to televise the Barons' games. The story mentioned that a play-by-play announcer was needed. "You should try out for the job," Michael's mom told him. "You'd be good at it." Michael, however, wasn't so sure. *The odds are against me*, he thought. *After all, I'm only nine years old.*

But the more he mulled the idea over, the more he thought he should at least give it his best shot. After all, what could he lose by trying?

To get himself ready for the tryout, Michael rigged up a hockey game on his computer. He made one team the Hanover Barons, using the real players' names. The other team would be the Philadelphia Flyers, he decided — his favourite NHL team. Michael practised his play-by-play three times a week on the computer. He read and reread all the Hanover players' names and statistics. He also phoned the number provided in the newspaper story and said he was interested in the job. "Come to a practice," he was told by Cal Harrington who worked at the hockey arena. "You can meet Mike Anderson."

When Michael Weber walked into the arena at the Barons' practice, Mike Anderson wasn't too sure what to think. A young boy wasn't exactly what the editor of the *Hanover Post* had in mind for a hockey announcer. But he was impressed by Michael's enthusiasm and how hard the boy had worked to prepare himself for the tryout. *The kid is definitely keen,* Mike Anderson thought to himself.

He talked it over with the others involved. "Should we put this much responsibility on a nine-year-old?" he asked them, worried. But no one could dispute the fact that Michael was certainly the keenest applicant they had. They decided that he deserved a chance to prove himself.

Over the next two months, Michael attended the Barons' training camp sessions, pre-season games, and practices. He pored eagerly over the stats and information that Mike Anderson provided, and peppered him with questions.

Michael also decided to create an audition tape out of a game that he and his mom liked to play. When they were driving in the car, Michael and his mother would do mock play-by-plays of an imaginary hockey game. They decided to tape-record one of their games and submit that recording along with Michael's tapes of exhibition games. Mike Anderson said he'd listen to the tapes and decide whether Michael had the right stuff.

The plan worked. Michael was invited to do the play-by-play for the first period of the Barons' first telecast home game of the regular season.

On November 3, 1995, Michael Weber got dressed in his only suit, got in the car with his mom and brother Jeff, and drove the 10 minutes to the Hanover Coliseum. Waiting for the game between the Barons and the Brussels Bulls to begin, Michael felt a little nervous. But when the referee dropped the first puck of the game, the words sprang easily to his lips. Everything he'd been studying suddenly became so important — the players' names and vital statistics, who the best players were, who would have the most ice time. . . . "And the Bulls win the draw," proclaimed Michael, and the game — and Michael's career — began.

Mike Anderson was amazed. And he wasn't alone. Any doubts lingering in the minds of the hockey team, the cable company executives, or the editor of the *Hanover Post* simply disappeared. *This nine-year-old kid is cool as a cucumber,* Mike thought. *He isn't fazed a bit.* "It looks like there's a penalty coming against the Barons," Michael said, seconds before the referees called a game misconduct against a Hanover player. "The Bulls, taking advantage of the power play, shoot it just wide of the net," he continued, his voice rising with excitement.

Mike Anderson asked Michael to stay and do the second period. Then he invited Michael back for a second game, and a third. Pretty soon, nine-year-old Michael Weber was the "Voice of the Hanover Barons."

Reporters clamoured to meet the young sportscaster. He appeared on *Midday*, *Behind the News*, *The National*, *Global News at Six*, and *Morningside With Peter Gzowski*. Classmates even began asking for his autograph. Still, Michael continued to work hard. He wanted to be even better — more polished, more familiar with other teams' players, more of a pro.

It wasn't easy. Michael had to juggle his new job with hockey practices of his own. He played on the town's Novice B team, the Hanover Lions, which won the trophy for its division. He also had to keep up with his schoolwork. His mom had made it very clear that school was Michael's first priority. Somehow, he even found time to write a speech about broadcasting, which he presented to his Grade 4 class at Mildmay Carrick Public School. He was one of only two students selected to present their speeches to the entire school.

With more and more people taking notice of Michael's talents, the future is looking bright for the young announcer. Still, if Michael has his way, he'll *play* in the NHL first, and *then* call the play-by-plays. He's already done some announcing with Craig Foster, a Junior A sportscaster.

But for now, Michael is happy to be the Voice of the Hanover Barons.

"We didn't give the job to Michael because he was a kid," says Mike Anderson. "We gave it to him because he was the best person for the job."

"FIRE!"

November 4, 1990, started out as a typical evening for five sisters in the Betts family in Niagara Falls, Ontario. Twelve-year-old Tiffiney Betts and her 15-year-old stepsister Miranda were looking after their three younger sisters while their father, stepmother, and uncle went to a party. They ordered in pizza, listened to music, and watched some television.

After tucking the three younger girls in bed, Tiffiney and Miranda popped the movie *Innerspace* into the VCR and settled down to watch. Tiffiney worked on a poem she was writing for a friend's upcoming birthday. By 1:30 a.m., the two girls were ready for bed themselves. They turned out the lights, crawled into their beds — Miranda on the top bunk, Tiffiney on the bottom — and fell sound asleep. Neither one heard the adults arrive home much later.

TIFFINEY BETTS

But something did wake Tiffiney up very early the next morning. When she opened her eyes, however, she couldn't see a thing. She rubbed them and blinked a few times — still nothing but blackness. What had woken her up? Suddenly, she smelled smoke and jumped out of her bottom bunk. *Oh, my God,* she thought to herself, *the house is on fire!* Because of her severe asthma, Tiffiney could think of only one thing — filling her burning lungs with fresh air.

With thick smoke filling the tiny bungalow Tiffiney's mind raced through her options. A pull-out bed against the front door made it impossible to open. That meant her only chance for escape was the side door off the kitchen — but the kitchen was three rooms away.

Tiffiney remembered the instructions of a fire prevention officer who had visited her class. He had warned the Grade 7 students that smoke kills before fire does. "Smoke also rises," he had cautioned them, "so crawl as close to the ground as possible." Blinded by the smoke and barely able to breathe, Tiffiney dropped to her hands and knees and crawled through the clutter of the living room, through the sitting room, through the kitchen, and out the side door. Once outside, she took deep, hungry breaths of cold fresh air. But while Tiffiney was safe, she suddenly realized that she was alone — everyone else was still inside the burning house.

Down the street glowed the lights of the all-night gas station on the next block. *I should run for help,* she told herself frantically. But she was afraid that help would arrive too late to save her sisters. With one last clear breath, she crawled back inside.

On her hands and knees, Tiffiney crawled back through the smoke-filled rooms to her bedroom. To reach Miranda, still asleep on the top bunk, Tiffiney had to stand up where the smoke was thickest. She could only just make out the shape of her stepsister in her bright yellow pajamas. Tiffiney shook her urgently. "Hmmph," Miranda mumbled, "leave me alone," and rolled over to go back to sleep.

"Miranda, *wake up!*" Tiffiney grabbed her stepsister's long brown hair and gave it a furious tug. Dazed but awake, Miranda slid off the top bunk and crawled after her sister through the living room, sitting room, kitchen, and out the side door.

As Tiffiney gasped in some fresh air, Miranda started crying. "Please don't cry," begged Tiffiney. She remembered the words of the fire prevention officer. "When there's a fire, always keep doors shut," he had told the class, explaining that closed doors help stop air from getting in and spreading the fire farther. "Keep the door shut, Miranda," ordered Tiffiney, and she disappeared back into the smoke.

Into the bedroom off the kitchen she crawled, where nine-year-old Bonnie shared her room with two-year-old Aleasha. Bonnie was just waking up. Tiffiney shook Aleasha awake. "Hold hands," she said to her two younger sisters. "I'll be right behind you."

The three sisters crawled to the kitchen. Barely visible through the smoke was the girls' father, sound asleep at the kitchen table. "Wake up," Bonnie begged her dad. The girls tried to shake him awake but he wouldn't stir.

"We've got to get out," Tiffiney urged her sisters. She saw that the smoke was sinking lower to the ground and she noticed flames in the living room. She was running out of time to get everyone out. The girls crept through the thick smoke out the side door. Again, Tiffiney tried to catch her breath. The crackle of flames was growing louder.

While her sisters huddled together on the lawn, Tiffiney went back again into the house. Inside, the fire was burning more fiercely. She could see flames all around the pull-out bed in the living room. And lying in the middle of the bed was Tiffiney's stepmother, Jean, her eyes closed, her face beaded with sweat. Leaping onto a yellow armchair, Tiffiney jumped over the ring of flames onto the bed. Grabbing her sleepy step-mom, she dragged her to the kitchen. "Help me get Dad," she demanded. Together, the two managed to carry Tiffiney's father outside and onto the lawn.

Just then, a window exploded right behind Tiffiney, sending shattered glass everywhere. Over the sound of Aleasha's terrified screams, the family could make out another sound — a baby crying. "Oh, my God," cried Jean. "Where's my baby?" Paralysed with fear, everyone stood still.

Tiffiney raged at herself for forgetting tiny Crystal, who had been fast asleep in her crib in Aleasha and Bonnie's room. Back into the burning house she crawled, fighting her way through the smoke into the girls' bedroom. Frantically, she clawed through the blankets in the crib. *She's not here!* thought Tiffiney in panic, when she couldn't feel any weight in the blankets. Where was her baby sister? Suddenly, she heard a muffled cry. Crystal was among the blankets! She picked the crying baby back up, held her close to her chest, and walked back out through the smoke. The heat was unbearable, and Tiffiney was suddenly exhausted. Out of the corner of her eye, she could see paint bubbling on the wall. Smoke had filled the house from floor to ceiling and suddenly every room was in flames. With Crystal in her arms, she ran outside for the last time.

Out on the lawn, the Betts family sat in horror as fire swallowed their home. There was no hope of going back inside. Barely able to run, Tiffiney made her way to the 24-hour Esso station down the street. Richard Bouchard, the 24-year-old attendant, was startled at the sight of the gasping 12-year-old, covered in cuts and soot. When he hurried outside, he could see flames reaching into the sky. Quickly, he dialled 911 and then ran to the Betts's home, with Tiffiney right behind him.

The family, dazed and terrified, sat huddled near the road, with neighbours gathering around them. "Uncle Harry is still inside," the children told the attendant. Jumping over the railing onto the front porch, he could see smoke billowing out from under the door. He could hear the flames and — worse — he could hear a man groaning. In spite of the shouts of warning, he managed to push the front door open with his shoulders. He disappeared into the house and returned moments later dragging the girls' uncle onto the front lawn. Uncle Harry was in bad shape.

With lights flashing, the fire trucks and ambulance arrived. Harry was quickly loaded into the ambulance and rushed to the hospital. Police urged Tiffiney and the rest of the family to get oxygen from the ambulance attendants, but they declined. Attendants did check them all over and, surprisingly, they were all fine. Harry wasn't so lucky. He died later that day in the hospital.

The family gathered at a neighbour's house to figure out what to do next. Not long after, Tiffiney's grandparents arrived. She fell into her grandfather's arms for a much-needed hug.

The next few days were a blur. Tiffiney couldn't

eat — everything tasted like smoke — and she had trouble sleeping

It was the police constable investigating the fire who first recognized the courageous act of young Tiffiney Betts. As a result, Tiffiney was honoured with bravery awards from the Niagara Regional Police and the Royal Canadian Humane Association. She also received the Star of Courage from the Governor General of Canada.

She's proud of her honours, but is modest about the role she played. "They're family members," she responds. "You should save them." In fact, she even got tired of all the attention she received after word of her heroics got out. However, to the rest of us, the bravery of a young girl with asthma who saved her family is nothing short of incredible.

THE FIRST OF MANY STEPS

On a cold day in May 1995, a father and his son waited in the freezing drizzle at the border between the provinces of Ontario and Manitoba. They were about to begin a four-month journey that would change many lives. Sherene Davidson kissed her husband and son good-bye. Then, with little fanfare but much determination, John Davidson, pushing his 15-year-old son Jesse in a wheelchair, took the first of four million steps that would take them across Ontario to raise money for research into genetic diseases. This father-and-son team knew first-hand the difficulties and pain that genetic diseases cause. Jesse has Duchenne muscular dystrophy — a disease that attacks the muscles of boys. As the muscles

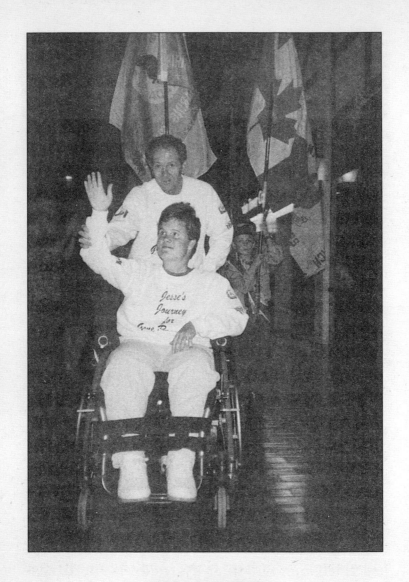

JESSE DAVIDSON

waste away, the boys slowly weaken and then die, often in their teens.

Although the physical part of the journey began that day, the hard work had begun more than a year earlier . . .

On April 10, 1994, Jesse Davidson and his father, John, went out to a local restaurant in their hometown of London, Ontario, to celebrate Jesse's 14th birthday. Jesse expected a quiet night out, but John had something very important he wanted to discuss.

"Are you crazy?" Jesse's dark eyes opened wide when his dad outlined his plan for the two of them to cross Ontario together — John on foot, Jesse in his wheelchair. They would raise money and awareness to help Jesse and others with genetic diseases.

"After all," John reminded his son, "look what Terry Fox and his Marathon of Hope did for cancer."

"What about school?" asked Jesse, who was in Grade 9 at Saunders Secondary School. "I'll have to be away for a long time." And, he questioned his father, where would they get the funding to support them? Where would they get supplies? Jesse also knew that such a journey would be very hard work.

John Davidson wasn't surprised at his son's reluctance. Jesse, a cautious, organized kid, liked to think things through. But even though Jesse wasn't immediately convinced, he soon became excited about the idea. It made him happy to realize that he would be raising money for a good cause and helping others like himself. John, Jesse, and the whole Davidson family were determined to fight this disease, and they needed money for research to help them. "I didn't want to be a role model," Jesse says now. "I just wanted to be someone who set a goal, and met it."

They set their financial goal at $1 million — to be donated to the newly formed Foundation for Gene and Cell Therapy. Then they got to work on "Jesse's Journey," as it was named — getting sponsors, raising funds, and recruiting volunteers to help with driving the donated motor home, talking with media, and acting as gofers. They also hired two assistants. Tricia Federkow, a kinesiologist, would tend to John's and Jesse's muscle aches and blisters, and would also take care of the practical matters such as where and when they would eat, and where they would stay overnight. Sean Bagshaw, a kinesiology student, would be Jesse's personal attendant. His job would be to look after Jesse's special physical needs. People with muscular dystrophy tire extremely easily, and everyone knew the trip would be particularly hard on Jesse.

Jesse's Journey began on a cold, lonely stretch of Northen Ontario highway, with only a few supporters to send them off. Both John and Jesse found it tough to get up every day and carry on. The roads were hilly and, in spite of that first freezing day, the summer was quickly becoming one of the hottest in years. "It was repetitive," says Jesse. "There were so many hills that were exhausting." Jesse had to be sure to get lots of rest. John, at 49 years old, was in good shape, but the 30 kilometres a day of walking took its toll on him as well. Still, each day, every day, they got up, put Jesse in his wheelchair, and pushed on, followed by the motor home carrying the assistants, volunteers, and all their supplies.

In Thunder Bay, John and Jesse came across a monument to Terry Fox, whose Marathon of Hope inspired people around the world. Jesse gazed up at the statue of Terry Fox, gathering strength from the runner's words. "Dreams are made if people only try," he read on the monument. "I believe in miracles. I have to, because somewhere the hurting must stop." For John, inspiration sat every day in front of him in a wheelchair.

The two picked up steam. They had already travelled more than 5,000 kilometres on their journey and people were starting to take notice.

It was a beautiful hot, sunny day when John and Jesse arrived in Powassan, Ontario. They had put 16,520 kilometres behind them and had roughly the same distance to go. "Jesse's Journey: Halfway Point" read the huge banner stretching across the road. John began to jog, and he and Jesse burst through the banner — or tried to. Instead of tearing, as planned, the banner wrapped itself around the excited pair. Laughing, they untangled themselves, and Jesse grinned and waved at the crowd. The streets of Powassan were filled with cheering people offering words of encouragement. Jesse was becoming a celebrity, and he happily signed small Canadian flags for the boys and girls who gathered around his wheelchair.

But even though there were many days filled with laughter and fun, Jesse and John were often reminded of their journey's purpose when they met people who had lost a family member or friend to a genetic disease.

Just outside of Wawa, Ontario, a woman approached Jesse and his father with an unusual favour. At her nearby farm, she had a 10-day-old colt that needed a name. Her 13-year-old daughter was supposed to name the colt, the woman explained, but she didn't live long enough. She had died of a genetic disease. "Please," the woman asked, "could Jesse name the colt?" With tears in their eyes, John and Jessie made their way to the farm and to the nameless colt. "Snowy," said Jesse, stroking the nose of the young horse with the snow-white blaze across its face. And Snowy it was.

By the time John and Jesse entered southwestern Ontario, their journey was gaining more attention. They were met by bigger crowds, they were collecting more money, and they were nearing their hometown of London, where they expected to see lots of their friends and supporters. Fifty-six kilometres outside of London, Jesse knew that they were getting close. "Hey, look," he said excitedly. "A 'London' sign."

On August 21, the day they'd been dreaming about arrived — and it couldn't have been better. Three months and 26,353 kilometres later, the two arrived to a thunderous welcome. Thousands of people lined the streets to offer warm wishes and cold hard cash to their hometown heroes. On that one day alone, Londoners donated more than $75,000 to research into genetic diseases.

To add to the wonderful day, Dianne Haskett, London's mayor, announced that a local park would be named Jesse Davidson Park. *Perfect*, thought John. *A park is a lasting tribute, something that can't be taken away.*

Back on the road again, John and Jesse saw Jesse's grandparents in Woodstock, and then travelled on to the big city of Toronto. Although the Torontonians weren't very generous with their money, the media welcomed the pair with open arms. They spent the day doing a number of television and newspaper interviews, telling people about their journey and what they hoped to achieve.

Jesse also loved visiting the Hockey Hall of Fame where hockey legend Darryl Sittler, a spokesperson for Jesse's Journey, presented him with a Toronto Maple Leafs hockey sweater. He even met famed hockey commentator Don Cherry. But for Jesse, a true baseball fan, the greatest thrill was to be invited onto the field at the SkyDome to wave to the many other fans of the Toronto Blue Jays — and of Jesse Davidson.

The next day they were on the highway early, but John and Jesse knew the end was near.

On September 20, 1995, more than 33,000 kilometres and four months had passed. Jesse's Journey had raised $800,000 — their goal was within reach. Just like on that first day in May, Mother Nature delivered drizzle. Still, the mood in Ottawa was festive, and Jesse and John were thrilled when Canadian Prime Minister Jean Chrétien met them on Parliament Hill. Afterwards, people cheered them along the last few kilometres of their long journey.

Finally, John and Jesse approached the finish line on the Québec side of the Alexandra Bridge. Underneath the wheels of Jesse's chair, the wooden planks of the bridge clacked loudly. John's pace quickened. Jesse burst through the banner, and suddenly all their hard work, aching muscles, long days, and blisters were worth it. "We did it," said Jesse quietly, a smile lighting up his face.

Three months later, with donations still coming in, Jesse's Journey reached its goal of $1 million for gene and cell research. May 20, the day the journey began, has become a day for families to do something special together to help raise more money. And it has become a day of hope for families and friends of those with genetic diseases. For Jesse, the journey was more than a chance to raise money for a very worthy cause. "I found out what I could do, what my abilities were," he says. "I found out that if I had a goal and I tried, at least I'd feel satisfied with what I did."

On September 26, 1996, Jesse and his father were awarded their province's highest honour — the Order of Ontario.